PUPPET
PROGRAMS
No. 2

29 Puppet Scripts for Children

by Marilyn Millikan

Lillenas Publishing Co.

KANSAS CITY, MO. 64141

Index

My Adopted Puppet Family

Nothing gets the attention of children more than a puppet or dummy!

Peter, a hand puppet made of felt, was my very first puppet. Complete with scripts he cost about $3.00 and can still be purchased in Bible bookstores. After using the prepared scripts, I began to write my own to go with the particular lesson I needed. Then, as director of vacation Bible school, I wanted something different to attract the children, so I invested $6.98 for a Danny O'Day dummy and a record on how to use ventriloquism. Danny was a real hit at Bible school and afterwards he became a regular attender of Sunday school and children's church. He is still around and makes appearances on request. A few years later I was visiting Disney World and found a girl counterpart to Danny. For $12.00 I acquired Susy and fixed up a blond wig for her. She was a real charmer and was a success with the children, but she and I didn't get along quite as well as Danny and I, since his low voice was much easier for me to do than her high voice.

When my children were small, Ivory Soap came out with a promotion in which storybook hand puppets were given away. I got these for my children and began to write scripts and use them in children's work, as well. Some of them were Tweetie Bird, Pedro Mouse, and the Wizard of Oz puppets. Boy and girl sack puppets came in our Sunday school literature and they have been important in my puppet ministry.

While visiting in the toy department of Marshall Fields in Chicago, I fell in love with a white fur bunny puppet. Seven dollars made her mine, and on the way home I developed her personality and named her Petunia Blossom. She made her first appearance at vacation Bible school and many times afterwards I would meet children on the street who wanted to know about "Tunia." She is still around and is a special favorite of young children.

Wanting to involve teens in our puppet ministry, I bought marionette puppets. They are much harder to work with and training is needed for the puppeteers. They can be purchased at toy stores for under $10.00. There are easy two-string puppets and the harder-to-use four-string ones. These are excellent for plays requiring several characters. Costumes can be made to change appearances.

Any hand puppet can be given a personality to relate to the boys and girls. The tin woodman Oz puppet became my Can Man and was easy to write scripts for.

Puppets need not be costly, but they should be made real by having a personality and character that a child understands. A number of these scripts were written with use of just one puppet or dummy. Others of the scripts involve several "people puppets." You can involve the children, too, by

4

having them use these dialogues for hand puppets. Though I have chosen names to use in my scripts, you may use any names you wish.

You will notice that Johnny is a sweet little boy, but very mischievous. He loves a good joke (and some of his are not so good!) and will get one in at the slightest suggestion. Don't be afraid of using jokes. This is an excellent way to get a child's attention. A laughing child is more eager to learn than a sober, indifferent child.

My puppets are part of my family! Yours can be, too, and as you begin to talk with them regularly a personality will surface and you will find simple scripts coming to mind which you can use in your classes.

We wish you happiness and success in your puppet ministry!

—MARILYN MILLIKAN

Pedro and Tweetie
Go to Junior Church

(Puppet dialogues for a bird, a mouse, a little girl, and a cat.)

TWEETIE—Hi! I'm Tweetie Bird. Are you Mighty Mouse?

PEDRO—Not quite. I'm Pedro Mouse. I'm from the West.

TWEETIE—Oh, I'm glad to meet you. Being from the wild west, I bet you are brave.

PEDRO—Well, I'm sorta brave. I'm still scared of cats, though.

TWEETIE—Oh, me, too. Say, Pedro, let's be friends and protect each other from the cats.

PEDRO—Sure, that will be great! What can we do now?

TWEETIE—I know, let's tell jokes. Do you know who was first to reach the moon?

PEDRO—Was it the astronaut?

TWEETIE—No. It was the cow. She jumped over it. Ha! Ha!

PEDRO—Pretty good. Say, what did one wall say to the other?

TWEETIE—Do you want me to hold you up?

PEDRO—No, silly, it said, "Meet you at the corner." *(laugh)*

TWEETIE—Say, Pedro, where are we anyway? I have been so busy watching out for the cat, I didn't notice where we were.

PEDRO—Oh, this is Junior Church. I've been here lots of times, peeking out from under the piano.

TWEETIE—What do they do here anyway?

PEDRO—Well, they sing and a lady tells a story.

TWEETIE—What's the story about?

PEDRO—Oh, about Jesus and the Bible and heaven and being good.

TWEETIE—Say, you mean this really is a church?

PEDRO—Sure. A church for kids.

TWEETIE—Do you think it's all right if I'm here? I don't know what to do.

PEDRO—You have to sit still and listen. No flying around all the time.

TWEETIE—Okay. What else?

PEDRO—You have to sing and pray when the others do.

TWEETIE—I can sing, but I've never prayed.

PEDRO—Just watch me. I've learned all about prayer. We pray to God in Jesus' name.

TWEETIE—What do we say in our prayer?

PEDRO—We ask God to help us be good, to help people who are sick, and to help us to love one another.

TWEETIE—That is great! What else do we do in church?

PEDRO—We give an offering—money, you know. And then there are some things we don't do.

TWEETIE—What's that?

PEDRO—Like I said, we don't make noise. We don't bother other people and we are supposed to listen to our director. Think you can follow all those rules?

TWEETIE—Sure. I'm going to like Junior Church. Do you suppose I could come all the time? A silly bird like me?

PEDRO—Yes! Anyone can come. Let's you and me sneak over here and sit still and you can find out more about Junior Church.

TWEETIE—Oh, boy; oh, boy!

Pedro and Tweetie Meet Jill

TWEETIE—Hi there, Pedro.

PEDRO—Hi, Tweetie. I'm all out of breath. I've been running from Kitty Kat.

TWEETIE—Oh. Oh. Kitty Kat around here? I'm leaving.

PEDRO—Hold on a minute. Kitty Kat ran the other way. He saw another mouse and chased him. I don't know what I'm going to do about that cat.

TWEETIE—We've got to think of a way to get rid of him, that's all.

PEDRO—Maybe a car will run over him or something. I'm sure afraid of that Kitty.

JILL—Hi, Tweetie and Pedro. Remember me? I go to the church you visited the other day.

PEDRO—Hi, Jill. Have you seen that Kitty Kat around?

JILL—Why, yes, on my way I saw a very nice kitty who stopped to let me pet him.

TWEETIE—Oh, you shouldn't have done that. He is a mean kitty.

JILL—No, he was very nice. You must not know him very well.

TWEETIE—He tries to eat birds!

PEDRO—And mouses, too.

JILL—Maybe if you would become his friend, he wouldn't try to hurt you.

PEDRO—A friend to Kitty Kat! Oh my!

JILL—Why don't we try it? Come on, I'll go with you.

PEDRO—You won't let him hurt us?

JILL—Of course not. You know if we want someone for a friend we have to be friendly, too. Maybe Kitty Kat needs a friend.

PEDRO—But does it have to be us?

JILL—I learned in Sunday school that we should love everybody, even our enemies.

8

TWEETIE—It sure would be hard to love Kitty Kat.

JILL—You know what I'm going to do? I am going to help you be friends. I am going to talk to Kitty Kat and tell him what a nice mouse and bird you are.

PEDRO—Do you think he'll listen?

JILL—Sure, I think he will. I am going to tell him you want to be friends. So long, now, I'll look up Kitty Kat and then I will let you know what I've learned.

PEDRO—Bye, Jill. It sure would be nice to be his friend instead of his enemy.

TWEETIE—It sure would! Bye, Jill.

Pedro and Tweetie Meet Kitty Kat

PEDRO—Hey, there, Tweetie, do you know the difference between an elephant and a flea?

TWEETIE—Well, one is big and one is . . .

PEDRO—No, no. Elephants have fleas, but fleas can't have elephants. Ha! Ha!

TWEETIE—Pretty good, Pedro. Here's one. What kind of an animal has a head like a cat and a tail like a cat but isn't a cat?

PEDRO—I don't know.

TWEETIE—A kitten. *(laughs)* I fooled you. Say, have you seen Jill?

PEDRO—I've been watching for her. I wonder if she saw Kitty Kat? Maybe Kitty Kat ate her up.

TWEETIE—No, she's too big for Kitty Kat to eat. Hey, here she comes now and she's got Kitty Kat with her. Oh, oh, let's run!

JILL—Wait! Wait! We won't hurt you. Kitty Kat wants to be your friend.

TWEETIE—Are you sure?

JILL—Come on, Kitty Kat, tell them.

KITTY KAT—Sure, fellows, I want to be your friend. Jill told me what the Bible says about loving everybody.

JILL—And you know what, Kitty Kat never did want to hurt you, he just wanted to play.

PEDRO—Really? You just wanted to play and we thought you wanted to eat us up.

KITTY KAT—Yeh, I'm a good cat. I like birds and mice. I want to be friends.

JILL—How about it, fellows, will you be friends with Kitty Kat?

TWEETIE—It would be nice to have you to play with, Kitty Kat. One can't have too many friends.

KITTY KAT—I'll even protect you, since I'm the biggest.

TWEETIE—And I can sit up in the trees and let you know when the dog comes along.

PEDRO—And I can be your friend and help you, too.

JILL—This is wonderful, now that you are all friends. Wouldn't the world be a better place if everybody loved one another and were friends?

TWEETIE—It sure would. Come on, let's see who else we can be friends with.

Yes, You Can!

(Puppet show for a little girl and a tin woodman puppet)

CAN MAN—Hi, there everybody. I'm the Can Man. There is no other man like me in the whole wide world.

BETTY—Hey, Mr. Can Man, I'm Betty. Where did you come from?

CAN MAN—Why, I'm made from a can and I am strong. You can't hurt me if you hit me. Come on, try. Hit me!

BETTY—Oh, I don't want to hit you.

CAN MAN—It won't hurt. I don't have any blood or bones or skin. I don't have any feelings. But, I got eyes and I can see lots of things.

BETTY—Like what, Mr. Can Man?

CAN MAN—Well, I watch out for people who are in trouble and I try to help them.

BETTY—Have you ever helped anyone?

CAN MAN—Sure. Want to hear about it?

BETTY—Yes. I think it is wonderful to help someone.

CAN MAN—The other day I saw a big bully beating up on a little boy. I chased the boy away and he threw some rocks at me, but it didn't hurt. I'm the Can Man.

BETTY—What else did you do?

CAN MAN—Mrs. Smith was burning leaves in the yard and her little dog got in the flames and I jumped in and brushed off the fire. Fire won't hurt me.

BETTY—You sure are great. I wish I could do things to help people.

CAN MAN—You can. You are a girl, aren't you?

BETTY—But I don't have anything to help me like you do.

CAN MAN—You have eyes and ears and hands and legs, don't you?

BETTY—Sure. Everyone does.

CAN MAN—Use your legs to run errands for old people. Use your eyes to read to little children who are sick or need someone to play with. Use your lips to smile at people. Did you know that some people never see a smile?

BETTY—You mean I can really help people by doing those things?

CAN MAN—Yes, you can! And use those pretty hands to bake some cookies or candy for someone who is a shut-in. Use your hands to earn a little money to help someone who is poor.

BETTY—I can do that! Thank you, Mr. Can Man. I'm going now to find someone to help.

Honoring God's Name

LEADER—Hi, Johnny.

JOHNNY—Hi; and hello, everyone. Hello there, Dottie.

LEADER—Johnny, this isn't the place to flirt. Do you know anything about the third commandment as given by God?

JOHNNY—No, but I know what is best for bees.

LEADER—What?

JOHNNY—Hives. Ha! Ha! I fooled you.

LEADER—You always have a joke, don't you. Did you hear our lesson about honoring God's name?

JOHNNY—Sure did. I'm going to keep that rule, too.

LEADER—I'm glad. You must remember never to use God's name in fun or foolishly.

JOHNNY—Never, never. Hey, bend down a minute. *(whispers)*

LEADER—Oh, no, Johnny, that is swearing.

JOHNNY—Really? How about "Gosh"?

LEADER—That sounds too much like God, so we shouldn't use it.

JOHNNY—How about when someone does wrong and I ask God to damn him?

LEADER—That is swearing, Johnny, and we should never swear.

JOHNNY—What can a fellow say when he gets upset?

LEADER—The Bible says in Matthew 5:37 to let your yes be yes and your no, no; and we are not to say foolish words.

JOHNNY—I surely don't want to displease God.

LEADER—You know you can tell how smart a person is by their words.

JOHNNY—If I use a lot of slang, I guess that shows I'm not too smart.

LEADER—That's right. I know you are working on getting smart, too.

JOHNNY—Learning to honor God's name will help me, too. Good-bye.

LEADER—Good-bye, Johnny.

In Times of Trouble

(Dialogues for dummy or puppet and friend)

LEADER—Hi, Johnny, it's good to see you today.

JOHNNY—Hi. Hi, kids. Hi, David. Hi, Betty. Hi, everyone.

LEADER—What have you been doing lately, Johnny?

JOHNNY—Practicing my Spanish.

LEADER—I didn't know you knew any Spanish.

JOHNNY—Sure. I'm learning it in case I ever meet up with any kids who speak Spanish.

LEADER—You really are?

JOHNNY—*Si, señora.*

LEADER—What did you say?

JOHNNY—*Si, señora.* That's Spanish for "Yes, Madam."

LEADER—What else can you say, Johnny?

JOHNNY—*Mi Jesu' ama.*

LEADER—What does that mean?

JOHNNY—Jesus loves me.

LEADER—Yes, you are right. Jesus loves all the boys and girls here, too.

JOHNNY—That's what I'm going to tell the kids I meet who speak Spanish.

LEADER—That will be great. I don't understand how you can speak Spanish when I don't know any.

JOHNNY—I can do a few things for myself, you know.

LEADER—You can? Anyway, Johnny, how do you know Jesus loves you?

JOHNNY—He helps me when I get in trouble.

LEADER—Can you tell us about sometime He did help you?

JOHNNY—The other day I was going home and it was getting dark.

LEADER—You were all alone?

JOHNNY—Yes, and some guy started to follow me.

LEADER—Were you scared?

JOHNNY—I sure was, but I remember that scripture in the Bible.

LEADER—When Jesus says, "Call on Me and I will answer"?

JOHNNY—That's the one. And also the one where it says that when we are afraid, to remember Jesus.

LEADER—So what did you do?

JOHNNY—I prayed for Jesus to help me get home safely.

LEADER—And you did get home, too. I was there.

JOHNNY—When I prayed there was a man and woman I knew who came down the side street and they walked with me the rest of the way home.

LEADER—That is wonderful, Johnny. I hope all the boys and girls will remember that Jesus loves them and that He will help them when they need Him.

JOHNNY—*Si, si.*

LEADER—Does that mean, Yes, yes?

JOHNNY—*Si.* I mean, yes.

LEADER—Sure nice to have you here today, Johnny. *Adios.*

JOHNNY—*Adios, amigos.*

Promoting Vacation Bible School

LEADER—Hi, there, Johnny. Sure nice to see you today.

JOHNNY—Hi.

LEADER—Why Johnny, what is the matter? You sound down in the dumps.

JOHNNY—I am.

LEADER—How come?

JOHNNY—Pretty soon school will be out and I won't have anyone to play with. I won't have any fun.

LEADER—Don't you have some friends that live in your neighborhood?

JOHNNY—No. I'm the only kid in my block.

LEADER—That is too bad. Say, I know.

JOHNNY—What? What?

LEADER—Why don't you come to vacation Bible school?

JOHNNY—What's that?

LEADER—You know. All the kids come to church and we learn about the Bible, and play games and do all kinds of interesting things.

JOHNNY—Really? What else do they do?

LEADER—They have Kool-Aid and cookies.

JOHNNY—Oh, boy. That settles it. I'm coming for sure.

LEADER—Wait. Don't you want to hear what else there is?

JOHNNY—You mean there's more?

LEADER—We have craft projects and they are great!

JOHNNY—What's that?

LEADER—Oh, we make animals, pictures, wood projects, and other things.

JOHNNY—Could I, too?

LEADER—Of course. And we have music, too. Maybe you could sing with the kids. You might even get to be soloist.

JOHNNY—Yeh, I like to sing. Boy, I'm coming to Bible school for sure. When is it?

LEADER—June 1-12, 9:00 to 11:30 in the morning.

JOHNNY—Ten whole days!

LEADER—No, just 10 half-days.

JOHNNY—I can't wait to come. Say, maybe I could tell the kids in Bible school one of my jokes.

LEADER—Like what?

JOHNNY—Do you know why the little boy put a frog in his sister's bed?

LEADER—No, why?

JOHNNY—He couldn't find a mouse.

LEADER—That is a new one for me.

JOHNNY—Hey, I saw an elephant skin the other day.

LEADER—Where was it?

JOHNNY—On the elephant. Ha! Ha!

LEADER—You had better save the rest for Bible school. We'll see you around.

JOHNNY—Okay. Bye, kids.

Jealousy

LEADER—Hi, Johnny.

JOHNNY—Hi. Hi, all you kids out there.

LEADER—How's school? Are you learning anything yet?

JOHNNY—No, I have to go back tomorrow. *(Pause.)* I learned a riddle.

LEADER—Let's hear it.

JOHNNY—Four girls walked to school under an umbrella but they didn't get wet. Why?

LEADER—I don't know. Was it a big umbrella?

JOHNNY—It wasn't raining. Ha! Ha!

LEADER—Do you remember the story about Cain and Abel, Johnny?

JOHNNY—Sure, it's in the Bible. Cain killed his brother Abel.

LEADER—Cain killed his brother because of jealousy. Do you know what that means?

JOHNNY—Cain thought God liked Abel better than him. I don't like that story very much.

LEADER—Why not?

JOHNNY—It reminded me of me once.

LEADER—What happened to you?

JOHNNY—This kid next door had a new 10-speed bike.

LEADER—Well?

JOHNNY—I wanted one, too, and I got so I didn't like him because he had a 10-speed and I didn't.

LEADER—So what did you do?

JOHNNY—One day I noticed our paper boy delivered his papers on foot. He didn't even have any bike and I did have a regular bike.

LEADER—You mean you saw that you were better off than you thought?

JOHNNY—I realized that the way I thought about the kid with the 10-speed was wrong. I could get along fine with what I had.

LEADER—I'm glad you forgot about the bike, Johnny. Did you become better friends with your neighbor?

JOHNNY—Sure, we are real good chums now.

LEADER—Maybe someday you'll get a 10-speed. But you may have to work to earn it.

JOHNNY—That's an idea. Be seeing you.

LEADER—Good-bye, Johnny.

Being a Helper

LEADER—Hi, Johnny. How are you today?

JOHNNY—I'm fine. How are all you kids?

LEADER—Say, Johnny, I heard you had to stay after school every day this week. What do you have to say for yourself?

JOHNNY—I'll sure be glad when it is Friday.

LEADER—Do you have a joke for the kids today?

JOHNNY—Do you know what the boy said when the farmer found him in the apple tree?

LEADER—No, what?

JOHNNY—He said one of the apples fell down and he was just putting it back.

LEADER—Johnny, the boys and girls have been studying about working in the church.

JOHNNY—Say, that's great. I sure would like to be a worker, too. Let's see, what can I do? I guess I couldn't be the preacher.

LEADER—No, not yet, anyway. And you are too young to be a teacher.

JOHNNY—Let's see. I could help the janitor. I could pick up paper and messy things kids leave around.

LEADER—You sure could, Johnny. That would be a big help and would be helping the church, too.

JOHNNY—And I could help the teacher keep our room neat. Some kids sure are messy.

LEADER—That would be good. You could bring boys and girls to church, too.

JOHNNY—Yes, and I could sing in the kids' choir. Couldn't I?

LEADER—Can you sing, Johnny?

JOHNNY—Sure. I know a song about building the church, too.

LEADER—I believe I know that one. It is about building the Temple, and *temple* means "church."

JOHNNY—As we all work together we can build the church. But if one of us lays down on the job, we can't build as good a church.

LEADER—You sing the song for us Johnny, and then we can all sing it together.

JOHNNY—"Building up the temple, building up the temple, building up the temple of the Lord. Brother, won't you help us, Sister won't you help us, building up the temple of the Lord."

LEADER—That was good, Johnny. Now, let's all sing it together.

JOHNNY—I must go, kids. I'll see you around. Good-bye.

LEADER—Good-bye, Johnny.

Sharing

LEADER—Hi, there. How are you, Johnny?

JOHNNY—Okay. How are you?

LEADER—I'm fine, too. In fact, I feel real good because I am going to do a good deed today.

JOHNNY—What are you going to do?

LEADER—I'm going to take a box of groceries over to Mrs. Smith. She has been shut in and can't get out. Then I am going to take her some books and sewing to do, too.

JOHNNY—What do you get for doing it?

LEADER—Nothing. Just the joy it gives me.

JOHNNY—Nothing? You're doing all that for nothing!

LEADER—Of course, it makes me feel good to help others.

JOHNNY—How come?

LEADER—Well, Jesus said to love everybody. He said for us to share our things with people who don't have much.

JOHNNY—I remember that in the Bible. I remember about the boy who shared his lunch.

LEADER—Do you remember what happened? Can you tell us?

JOHNNY—He had some fish and bread and he gave it to Jesus to feed the crowd.

LEADER—And Jesus told all the people to sit down on the ground and He took the food and gave thanks to God for it.

JOHNNY—And then the disciples passed out the food and there was enough to feed 5,000 people. That was a real miracle.

LEADER—It certainly was. Jesus did that miracle. But He couldn't have done it without the little boy sharing his lunch.

JOHNNY—Is that why you are sharing?

LEADER—Jesus needs our hands and feet to help Him do His work here on earth. But I enjoy helping others. It makes me feel good. Would you like to come with me?

JOHNNY—Sure, but I don't have anything to give.

LEADER—You can sing a song. She loves to hear children sing.

JOHNNY—Yes, I could. And I will tell her a joke to cheer her up. How about this one. Why are promises like fat ladies who faint in church?

LEADER—I don't know.

JOHNNY—Because they should be carried out immediately.

LEADER—She'll like that, Johnny. Maybe you can think of another joke, too. Shall we go?

JOHNNY—Okay. Good-bye, kids.

Salt

LEADER—Johnny, what do you have a box of salt for?

JOHNNY—I'm going to catch a bird.

LEADER—Catch a bird with a box of salt?

JOHNNY—Sure, haven't you heard? Just put salt on its tail.

LEADER—Have you thought how you are going to get close enough to the bird to put salt on its tail?

JOHNNY—No, I hadn't.

LEADER—Do you know what salt is good for?

JOHNNY—It makes things good to eat.

LEADER—It does. Food wouldn't taste good without salt. You know Jesus said that we Christians could be like salt.

JOHNNY—Like salt? What did He mean?

LEADER—He said we are the salt of the earth. Once again, what does salt do?

JOHNNY—It makes food good.

LEADER—Do you suppose that Jesus meant for Christians to make the world good, a better place to live?

JOHNNY—Just like salt makes food better, then we can make people feel better.

LEADER—Can you think of ways we can help people feel better?

JOHNNY—We can be kind and helpful.

LEADER—We can help the poor and visit the sick.

JOHNNY—We can give money for missions.

LEADER—We can help our parents.

JOHNNY—I get it. A good Christian is like salt, good for others.

LEADER—That's right, Johnny. Thanks for coming today. Say, what about the pie-eating contest you entered. How did you do?

JOHNNY—The other guy came in first and I came in sick.

LEADER—Oh, Johnny, you are funny. Good-bye now.

JOHNNY—Good-bye kids.

Walking on the Water

*(For boy and girl puppets with story visualized in
pictures or flannelgraph)*

BILL—Hi, kids! Boy, oh, boy, do we have a good story for you today. And it's true, every bit of it.

TOM—If it's about Jesus, of course it's true.

LISA—This story proves that He is Lord. He is Lord of the whole universe.

BETTY—We're going to sing a song to let you know what it's all about.

SONG—"Here Comes Jesus, Walking on the Water"*

BILL—When our story begins, Jesus had been preaching all day to the people.

TOM—The crowds just followed Jesus everywhere. He couldn't even have a coffee break. He was so busy.

---

*From *Sing and Celebrate.*

LISA—The mothers with their kids came to show them to Jesus. And the teens crowded around wanting to be just like Him. Everyone pushed and shoved to get a glimpse.

BETTY—Jesus got so tired that He told His disciples that He was going up into the mountain to pray.

TOM—"You disciples," He said, "get into your ship and go on over to the other side of the lake and I will come later."

BILL—The disciples finally got rid of the crowd by telling the folk that Jesus would be on the other side of the lake.

BETTY—The disciples got into their boat to sail across the lake. The crowd wanted to get in, too, but there wasn't room.

LISA—Peter and the others soon cast off and a wind blew up and out across the lake they went.

BILL—You know, kids, Lake Galilee is very beautiful but sometimes great storms will come up in a hurry.

TOM—And this was one of those times.

LISA—The wind started to blow and the clouds went over the sun.

BETTY—It got dark, very dark.

TOM—The waves began to get a little higher.

BILL—And higher.

LISA—And higher and higher.

BETTY—The disciples held on to their seats.

TOM—And their coats.

BILL—And their hats.

BETTY—It looked as though it was night. No moon shone. No stars.

LISA—It was so dark and they were so afraid.

TOM—Were they afraid!

BILL—They thought they were going to sink.

BETTY—The waves began to rock the boat harder and harder.

LISA—And harder.

BILL—I am sure they started to pray.

TOM—"Oh, if Jesus had just come with us," they might have said.

BETTY—"Are we ready to die?" they might have thought.

LISA—Harder and harder they rowed.

TOM—But it didn't help.

BILL—Rocking and turning, the little boat went out of control.

21

LISA—Water began filling the bottom of the boat.

BETTY—Using a bucket they bailed out the water in the boat.

TOM—But the water came in faster than it went out.

BILL—Death was upon them, they just knew it.

BETTY—Suddenly, they saw something!

LISA—"A light!" shouted Peter.

BILL—"Land!" cried John.

LISA—"A ghost!" whispered Andrew as the light got closer.

BETTY—"A ghost," repeated John. "No, we don't believe in ghosts."

TOM—"Then it is a spirit," they said, more frightened than ever.

BILL—"It's not a man because it's walking on the water."

BETTY—"Oh," they cried, "first the storm and now this. O God, help us."

LISA—Just then the Person walking on the water spoke.

BILL—"It is I. Be not afraid."

TOM—It was Jesus.

BETTY—"Yes, it is Jesus," they cried.

LISA—Peter got so excited that he jumped overboard and started walking toward Jesus.

TOM—Right on the water!

BILL—Reaching out to Jesus.

LISA—Keeping his eyes on Jesus.

BETTY—Then Peter realized what he was doing.

TOM—Yeh . . . he was walking on the water!

BILL—Walking on *the water!*

LISA—Peter looked down and saw the waves and thought . . .

BETTY—"What am I doing? I can't walk on the water!"

BILL—Peter began to sink in the water.

TOM—Now he was scared. I mean *scared!*

BETTY—"Lord, help me! Save me! I'm drowning!"

LISA—The Lord Jesus reached out His hand and took hold of Peter's.

TOM—He lifted Peter up and Peter wasn't afraid anymore. He had his hand safe in Jesus' hand.

BILL—Jesus said, "Peter, where is your faith? Can't you believe in Me?"

BETTY—Then Peter and Jesus walked to the boat. On the water!

LISA—They climbed into the boat.

TOM—And the wind stopped.

BILL—The waves calmed down.

LISA—There was peace. Jesus brought joy and took away their fear.

BETTY—Yes, He is Lord. He is real. He is Lord of all.

Helping Friends

LEADER—Hello, Johnny Jingle. What's new today?

JOHNNY—Not much. I got a new riddle. Made it up myself.

LEADER—Let's hear it.

JOHNNY—What is white and soft and falls down all the time?

LEADER—Could it be a kitten?

JOHNNY—It's snow.

LEADER—Of course, white and soft and falls. That is good.

JOHNNY—What has a tongue that is loose at both ends?

LEADER—I don't know.

JOHNNY—A woman. She talks all the time. Ha! Ha!

LEADER—That isn't so funny. I know some boys who talk all the time, too.

JOHNNY—Say, I've got a problem.

LEADER—What is it?

JOHNNY—You know Teddy, the boy who lives down the street from me? He's got a broken leg and can't walk for a while. I've been wanting to take him to see our Little League play ball. But how can we get him there?

LEADER—Can't you get someone to drive him there in a car?

JOHNNY—We've tried, but everyone is busy in the daytime.

LEADER—Why don't you and your friends carry him there?

JOHNNY—We thought about that, but it would hurt him too bad.

LEADER—Do any of you have a wagon?

JOHNNY—We sure do. That's an idea. We can put him in the wagon and pull him there and he can sit on the grass and watch the game. Say, thanks.

LEADER—This reminds me of the story in the Bible when the four friends brought their crippled friend to Jesus. When they got to the house where Jesus was, the crowd was so big that they couldn't get their friend close to Him.

JOHNNY—I remember. They wanted Jesus to heal him.

LEADER—The four friends carried the man on his bed to the roof. Then they let him down through the roof right at Jesus' feet.

JOHNNY—And Jesus healed the man and told him to take up his bed and walk.

LEADER—You boys will be helping your friend when you take him to the ball game. This is a good Christian thing to do.

JOHNNY—I have to go now and tell the fellows. Thanks a lot. Good-bye.

LEADER—Good-bye, Johnny.

When Sally Needed Help

(For two girl puppets)

Scene I: Two girls meet.

JULIE—Hi, Sally. What'cha doing?

SALLY—Hi. Nothing.

JULIE—Say, my brother told me a joke. Why did the hen go just halfway across the road?

SALLY—I don't know.

JULIE—She wanted to lay it on the line.

SALLY—That's funny, Julie.

JULIE—Then why didn't you laugh?

SALLY—I don't feel much like laughing.

JULIE—How come?

SALLY—My mother's sick and I'm worried about her.

JULIE—What's wrong?

SALLY—I don't know and the doctor doesn't either.

JULIE—Why don't you pray about it, like our Sunday school teacher said?

SALLY—Oh, that won't help.

JULIE—Have you ever tried it?

SALLY—No. It's okay for the pastor and Sunday school teacher and grown-ups to pray, I guess.

JULIE—Our Sunday school teacher said we could pray, too, and Jesus would hear our prayers.

SALLY—I wouldn't know what to say.

JULIE—It says in the Bible to just ask. Just ask Jesus.

SALLY—You mean just ask Jesus to help my mother get well?

JULIE—Sure. You know, once I tried to find someone to come with me to Sunday school for a contest and everyone I asked was either too busy or already attended some place.

SALLY—What did you do?

JULIE—I just prayed about it. I asked Jesus to help me find someone to ask because I was doing my very best.

SALLY—Did you find someone?

JULIE—The very next day two little girls came to spend the summer at the neighbor's and I invited them.

SALLY—Did they come?

JULIE—They sure did. Every Sunday that summer.

SALLY—Do you really think Jesus would hear my prayers?

JULIE—Our teacher says that if we really mean the words we say and then trust Jesus He will answer in the way He thinks is best.

SALLY—O Julie, I'm going right home and pray for mother. You pray, too, will you?

JULIE—Sure, Sally, and I know Jesus will help her get well.

Scene II: Two girls meet again.

JULIE—Hi, Sally. I haven't seen you for a week. How are you?

SALLY—Oh, just fine, Julie, and guess what?

JULIE—What?

SALLY—You know my mother was sick. Well, I went home and prayed for her and asked Jesus to help her get well.

JULIE—Did she get well?

SALLY—The very next day the doctor came and gave her some more tests and he found out that something she had been eating was making her very sick. She had an allergy to it. So, now she doesn't eat that anymore.

JULIE—Jesus must have helped the doctor find out what was wrong.

SALLY—Yes, and mother is all well. I am so glad I prayed.

JULIE—Don't forget, Sally, we can pray to Jesus all the time and He will help us. In fact, we should pray to Him every day.

SALLY—I know that, and I am praying every day. Good-bye now.

JULIE—Good-bye, Sally.

The House on the Rock

LEADER—Hi there, Johnny. How are you?

JOHNNY—Fine. Do you know what a cactus is?

LEADER—It's a plant that . . .

JOHNNY—No. No. It is a big pin cushion. You almost spoiled my joke.

LEADER—You know so many jokes. If you just knew as much about school as you do about jokes . . .

JOHNNY—I learned this in school the other day. What is a pup tent?

LEADER—You learned about a pup tent?

JOHNNY—It's a dog house. Ha! Ha! Ha! One of the kids told me.

LEADER—What else have you been doing lately?

JOHNNY—I am getting ready to build a house. Will you help me?

LEADER—What kind of a house?

JOHNNY—One that won't fall down.

LEADER—The Bible tells about two men who built houses. One did a good job and the other a poor job.

JOHNNY—How come the difference? Maybe I can learn something.

LEADER—One man built his house on the sand.

JOHNNY—What happened?

LEADER—When it stormed, the wind and rain beat on the sand and washed it away and the house fell down.

JOHNNY—I guess he was a poor builder. What about the other?

LEADER—He built his house on a rock foundation. And when the storm came, he was safe inside and didn't have to worry about his house falling down.

JOHNNY—I had better build on a good, strong foundation.

LEADER—Jesus told that story to show us that we should build our lives on a good foundation, too.

JOHNNY—I know. We are supposed to build our lives with Jesus' help. We are to let Jesus help us with our problems and everything.

LEADER—Right. Jesus wants us to love Him and become strong Christians—Christians who won't fall down when everything seems to be against them. We can trust Jesus to help us.

JOHNNY—I'm going to build my house on rock and I am going to be sure to build my spiritual house on Jesus Christ, our Rock. Good-bye now, kids.

LEADER—Good-bye, Johnny.

Silly Willie

(For use with any puppet)

LEADER—Why Willie, you've been crying.

WILLIE—I ran into a big kid down the block and he called me Silly Willie.

LEADER—Why would he do that, Willie?

WILLIE—He says I'm a dummy. He says I can't speak for myself.

LEADER—You may be a dummy, but I love you, Willie, and the kids here do, too.

WILLIE—You know what I'm going to do? I am going to go back and call that old kid Sloppy Joe. His name is Joe and he is sloppy, too.

LEADER—No, Willie, I don't think that would do. Jesus says we are supposed to turn the other cheek.

WILLIE—Even when someone calls you Silly Willie?

LEADER—Even if someone calls you bad names.

WILLIE—How come?

LEADER—Jesus says that a Christian is to be kind and good. We are never to hurt anyone.

WILLIE—Even if they hurt us?

LEADER—Just because someone else is bad doesn't mean a Christian should be bad, too. If we are followers of Jesus we will act like Jesus would.

WILLIE—How can we do this?

LEADER—We can ask Jesus to help us love everyone. And if we show love to others, pretty soon they are going to love us in return.

WILLIE—I never thought of that. I think I will try it.

LEADER—You will find out it will work, too. Willie, why don't you tell us a joke? It will make you feel better.

WILLIE—Here's one. What is a flood?

LEADER—Well, the water . . .

WILLIE—No, no. A flood is a river that's too big for its bridges.

LEADER—That is pretty good.

WILLIE—Did you hear about the boy who was thrown off the baseball team because he was honest?

LEADER—That seems strange.

WILLIE—He wouldn't steal bases. Ha! Ha!

LEADER—Come back again and see us. Will you, Willie?

WILLIE—I sure will. Good-bye, kids.

About Christmas

LEADER—Hi, Johnny, how are you today?

JOHNNY—I'm fine. But I'm trying to find out about Christmas. I've got to get a red suit and a beard.

LEADER—Why a red suit and a beard?

JOHNNY—Doesn't that mean it's Christmas?

LEADER—Oh, no. The person wearing a red suit and a beard is Santa Claus. He just has to do with presents. But that isn't really what Christmas is about.

JOHNNY—I heard some kids say they were buying lots of presents. Is that Christmas?

LEADER—Sometimes we give presents at Christmas to show our love, but that isn't the real meaning of Christmas.

JOHNNY—How about if I go out and sing songs for people? Is that Christmas?

LEADER—We do sing carols at Christmas, but that isn't the real meaning of Christmas either.

JOHNNY—I know. If I get a stocking and hang it up that will be Christmas.

LEADER—No, I'm afraid not, Johnny.

JOHNNY—I hear people talking about a Baby in a manger. Is that Christmas?

LEADER—Right! If it hadn't been for that Baby, we wouldn't be having Christmas.

JOHNNY—Who was that Baby?

LEADER—The Baby was Jesus Christ our Lord. He is the Son of God. God sent Him to earth as a baby to help us.

JOHNNY—How could He help us?

LEADER—The baby Jesus was to save us from our sins. He grew up to be a man and died for our sins.

JOHNNY—Why did God send His Son to do a thing like that?

LEADER—Because He loves us. He loves us so much that He sent His Son, Jesus, into the world. Whoever believes in Him shall have everlasting life.

JOHNNY—Then the Baby in the manger is Jesus and we worship Him?

LEADER—Yes. The songs we sing are about the Baby who loved us so much. That is the real meaning of Christmas. Jesus was God's Gift to us.

JOHNNY—Is that why we give presents to others at Christmas?

LEADER—Yes, and this helps us remember the very first Christmas Gift, Jesus our Lord.

JOHNNY—I am glad I know about the true meaning of Christmas. I am going to worship Jesus this Christmas.

LEADER—I am glad, Johnny, and I am going to worship Him, too. Good-bye now.

The Lost Sheep

(For boy and girl puppets and lamb puppet)

BOB—Say, kids, we're supposed to tell a Bible story today.

JEAN—Oh, boy, I just love Bible stories. Are you going to tell the story, Bob?

BOB—Not me. I think it's your turn, Jim.

JIM—No, I'm not prepared. Jean, you will have to tell the story.

JEAN—Not me. Listen, someone has to tell the story. Everyone is looking at us.

LAMB *(offstage)*—Baaa! Baaa! Baaa!

BOB—Wait, do you hear something?

JEAN—Sounded like a lamb to me.

JIM—There's no lamb in here. Must be a baby crying.

LAMB *(offstage)*—Baa! Baa! Baaaaaa!

JIM—I hear it again. Let's look around. *(Look around. Bob leaves.)*

BOB—Hey, here it is. It is a lamb! *(Comes onstage with lamb.)*

JEAN—Oh, I've never seen a lamb at church.

BOB—Come on, little fellow.

LAMB—I'm not a fellow. I'm Linda Lamb.

JIM—How did you get here anyway?

LAMB—My friend asked me to come to church and tell my story.

JEAN—You have a story? What about?

LAMB—It's about what happened to me. I was lost.

BOB—Really! That sounds like a good story. Let's hear it.

LAMB—You see, I was a little lamb and always stuck real close to my mother with all the other sheep. Mother always took care of me and didn't let the big rams bully me.

BOB—Sheep can be bullies, too?

LAMB—I'm afraid so. Anyway, I always had a good time, eating grass and drinking my mother's warm milk and sleeping and playing in the clover. But one day . . .

30

JEAN—Don't stop. What happened?

LAMB—One day there was a real bad storm and all the sheep crowded together hurrying to get through the fence to the barn.

JIM—And you got trampled?

LAMB—No, some of the big sheep pushed so hard they got between me and my mother and they just pushed her along with them toward the barn.

BOB—Did you find your way, then?

LAMB—Before I knew it the other sheep were gone and I couldn't keep up. It was beginning to get dark and I was afraid.

JEAN—I would be too. What did you do?

LAMB—I began to cry and run around looking for the way home. But, I couldn't find it.

JIM—Someone came to look for you, didn't they?

LAMB—The other sheep didn't care about just one little lamb like me, and my mother was already in the barn and couldn't get out to look for me.

BOB—I bet you were all wet.

LAMB—Just soaking. I was afraid I was going to drown. It was so wet and cold. Finally I couldn't go any farther. I just lay down between some rocks and cried to myself. A long time passed.

JEAN—I know you thought it was the end.

LAMB—I was so tired and wet. I could hardly lift my head. Suddenly, I heard a voice: "Here little lamb, here little lamb."

JIM—Who was it?

LAMB—It was the shepherd. He had counted the sheep and found there were only 99 and there should have been 100. He knew I was lost and so he came out in the rain and darkness to look for me.

BOB—Looks like he would have waited until morning.

LAMB—No, he was afraid a wolf or bear would get me. He cared about me and didn't want me to be lost. When I heard his voice, I cried again. He came over and picked me up in his strong arms and carried me back to the barn to my mother. She was really glad to see me.

JEAN—That shepherd was certainly a good one.

LAMB—He is the best shepherd of all because he cared about me.

LEADER—Jesus is our Good Shepherd, and our true Friend. When we are lost in sin He knows all about us. He calls for us to give up our sinful ways and come to Him. Jesus loved us so much that He died on the Cross that we might live. Just as the shepherd looked for the lamb, so Jesus wants to rescue us. Will you accept Jesus as your Shepherd? He is the one to pray to, to trust in, to believe in. *(If it seems right, the adult leader could give an invitation for boys and girls to give their hearts to Jesus.)*

The Christmas Story

(For Johnny Jingle and Leader)

LEADER—Johnny, do you know why we have Christmas?

JOHNNY—Sure, to get presents.

LEADER—No, Johnny, we do get gifts but that isn't why we have Christmas.

JOHNNY—To get to have a big dinner?

LEADER—No, that isn't it either. Would you like me to tell you and the other kids why we have Christmas?

JOHNNY—Sure. I like stories.

LEADER—This is a true story—the most beautiful story in the world. A long time ago God looked down on the world and all the things and people He had made. He saw things that made Him very sad.

JOHNNY—Like people who were bad?

LEADER—It seemed like everyone was very sinful. People hated and stole and killed. The world was a very bad place.

JOHNNY—I guess God decided to get rid of everyone?

LEADER—No. He loved all the people whom He had made. They were His children. So He thought and thought and decided someone would have to teach them how to be better.

JOHNNY—So what did He do?

LEADER—He decided to send His only Son, Jesus, into the world. You see, Jesus was God. He was God's Son and lived in a beautiful place called heaven.

JOHNNY—You mean He was going to leave heaven and live in the mean world?

LEADER—God said He would send His only Son to save the world from its sins. And He knew that for people to believe in Jesus He would have to become one of them to feel how they felt and experience with them sadness, sickness, and sorrow.

JOHNNY—That must have been hard for Jesus.

LEADER—God said that Jesus would come into the world as a baby, and grow up as a little boy.

JOHNNY—Just like all kids, huh?

LEADER—Yes. So God looked around and found a woman named Mary to be Jesus' earthly mother. She lived in a town called Nazareth, and her husband's name was Joseph.

JOHNNY—You mean Jesus was going to be a little baby just like we were once?

LEADER—That's right. An angel came to Mary and told her she would be the mother of a Son, and the angel told Joseph he should call the baby Jesus. I don't know if Mary and Joseph realized exactly how important this was, but they began to get ready.

JOHNNY—And then the baby Jesus was born?

LEADER—Not quite. You see all of that country was ruled by the Romans and they decided to count everyone who lived in that country. They sent out a notice for everyone to go to his own hometown to be counted. Mary and Joseph's hometown was Bethlehem.

JOHNNY—How far did they have to go?

LEADER—It was several days' journey to get to Bethlehem from Nazareth. They didn't have cars but had to walk or ride a donkey.

JOHNNY—You mean they walked all that way?

LEADER—Yes. And when they got to Bethlehem so many people had come to get counted that there wasn't any place to stay.

JOHNNY—Why didn't they stay at a motel?

LEADER—They didn't have motels in those days. Just a few poor little hotels called inns that kept travelers. Finally Mary and Joseph knocked on the door of an inn. Mary was so weary.

JOHNNY—What did they do?

LEADER—The innkeeper told them he had no room at all. Not even on the floor. But he said he had a stable where the cows and sheep stayed. It was warm and there was hay to sleep on.

JOHNNY—Yeh, that would be fun.

LEADER—Not for adults, Johnny, and especially Mary. There was no place else to go, so they went to the stable and I imagine the innkeeper brought them some food. And that night, the baby Jesus was born and they laid him in the manger for there was no room in the inn.

JOHNNY—Oh, boy, I wish I had been there.

LEADER—That would have been exciting. About that time out on the hills, the shepherds were taking care of their sheep.

JOHNNY—At night when it was dark?

LEADER—Yes, the shepherds had to stay with the sheep all night to protect them from wolves and robbers. While the shepherds were around the campfire and the sheep asleep, suddenly, suddenly, there was a great light in the sky.

JOHNNY—Oh, boy!

LEADER—The shepherds were scared. They fell on the ground and hid their faces. Soon, they heard a voice saying, "Fear not, for, behold, . . . unto you is born this day in the city of David, a Saviour, which is Christ the Lord."*

JOHNNY—Was that an angel voice?

LEADER—Yes, it was and then there were many, many voices in a giant choir singing glory to God.

JOHNNY—Angels singing! I wish I could hear that.

LEADER—Me, too. Finally the angels went away and the voices stopped. The shepherds didn't wait one minute. They said, "Let us go now into Bethlehem, and see this thing which has come to pass, which the Lord has made known to us."

JOHNNY—They were going to see the Baby, weren't they?

LEADER—The Lord must have directed them to the right place, for they entered the stable and saw the baby Jesus, and Mary His mother, and Joseph. They knelt and worshipped Him, for they knew that this was God come down to earth.

JOHNNY—Did they stay with the baby Jesus always?

LEADER—I am sure they wanted to, but they said, "Let us go and tell others of this wonderful thing that has come to pass."

JOHNNY—I bet everyone in Bethlehem wanted to see the Baby.

LEADER—The Bible doesn't say, but I imagine many others came to see Him. There is more to our story. Far away in an Eastern country some rich wise men saw a bright and beautiful star which they had never seen before. They wanted to find out about this star so they loaded their camels and started out to follow the star.

JOHNNY—How did they know where they were going?

LEADER—These men were called wise because they studied the stars and they knew this one was unusual. They had also been reading the Scriptures and knew that a king was to be born.

JOHNNY—The baby Jesus was our King.

LEADER—Yes, He is the King of kings and Lord of lords. Finally the wise men came to Jerusalem and went in to see Herod, the king. They asked Herod, "Where is He that is born King of the Jews? We have seen His star in the east and have come to worship Him."

JOHNNY—Did Herod know about the Baby?

LEADER—No. King Herod was angry. He was jealous, but he didn't let the wise men know it. He thought to himself that this might be a king who would grow up and take his throne away from him. He decided he must find this new King at once. He told the wise men to go and find the Baby

---

*Some scripture quotations are paraphrased from the KJV.

and then return and tell him where the Baby was so that he, Herod, could go and worship Him, too.

JOHNNY—He was lying, wasn't he?

LEADER—Yes, for Herod was a wicked king. The wise men followed the star till it came over the house where the baby Jesus was. They bowed down and worshipped the Baby and gave Him gifts of gold, frankincense, and myrrh. Then they left.

JOHNNY—Did they go back to Herod?

LEADER—The Lord told them to go back home another way, because Herod wanted to harm the baby Jesus. The Lord protected Jesus so He could grow up to become our Savior. And we have Christmas to celebrate the birth of the baby Jesus who came to earth to save us from our sins.

JOHNNY—That is a wonderful story.

LEADER—The most wonderful part is that if we believe that Jesus really was the Son of God, and that He died for our sins and rose again from the grave, then we can be saved and we can go to heaven to be with Him one day.

JOHNNY—Oh, I believe in Him!

LEADER—We must not only believe, but we must do what He wants us to do. We must live every day for Jesus.

JOHNNY—I am sure going to. That was a great story. I am glad I know the true meaning of why we have Christmas.

Children Can Pray

LEADER—Hello, Johnny, we are glad you are here today.

JOHNNY—I'm glad to be here. I like to be where there are a lot of kids.

LEADER—What have you learned since the last time we saw you?

JOHNNY—I've learned a new joke. Want to hear it?

LEADER—Okay.

JOHNNY—Why did the little boy throw the clock out the window?

LEADER—I don't know.

JOHNNY—He wanted to see time fly.

LEADER—What else have you learned?

JOHNNY—Not much. I have a question for you, though.

LEADER—Let's hear it.

JOHNNY—Are carrots really good for your eyes?

LEADER—Of course. Did you ever see a rabbit wearing glasses?

JOHNNY—Good for you. Say, I heard you talking about worship. Does God really see us when we worship?

LEADER—Of course. God is everywhere and He can always see us.

JOHNNY—We can't sing very good or pray very well.

LEADER—God looks at your heart or the way you feel on the inside. As long as we mean what we say, then God knows we are worshiping in our own way.

JOHNNY—I peeked when we prayed. Did God see that?

LEADER—Yes, He did. He probably saw you weren't really praying.

JOHNNY—I'm sorry and I am going to pray for sure, next time.

LEADER—I know you will and I hope all of us will do the same.

JOHNNY—I have to go now. See you next week, kids. Good-bye.

LEADER—Good-bye, Johnny.

The New Year

JOHNNY—Hello there, everybody.

LEADER—Hello, Johnny. How are you?

JOHNNY—Fine. I know what day this is.

LEADER—So do I. It's Sunday.

JOHNNY—No, it's more than that.

LEADER—Well, what is it?

JOHNNY—It's the first Sunday of our new year.

LEADER—You're right. It is.

JOHNNY—You know what you're supposed to do, too.

LEADER—What?

JOHNNY—You're supposed to make New Year's resolutions.

LEADER—I didn't make any. I was afraid I couldn't keep them.

JOHNNY—I made some. Want to hear them?

LEADER—I sure do.

JOHNNY—I am going to be good all year long.

LEADER—Are you sure?

JOHNNY—Sure I'm sure. And I'm never going to miss church.

LEADER—Oh, that is good. I wish all the boys and girls here would make that resolution. Then we would always have a big crowd.

JOHNNY—Hey, kids, let's all be good and plan to be in church every Sunday this year.

LEADER—Do you think they could come every Sunday?

JOHNNY—Sure, if they don't get sick.

LEADER—I think I will make that resolution, too, Johnny. I am going to be in church every Sunday.

JOHNNY—How about it, kids?

LEADER—That will be wonderful.

JOHNNY—Don't forget, kids. Join the 52 club and be present all the 52 Sundays of this year.

LEADER—Ask us again after 52 Sundays and see if we've all been here.

JOHNNY—I will. Say, do you use toothpaste?

LEADER—Of course. Do you?

JOHNNY—What for? None of my teeth are loose.

LEADER—After that, you will have to sit down. Good-bye now.

JOHNNY—Good-bye, everyone.

Mary Buys a Christmas Present

(A play for hand puppets or marionettes)

Scene I

(Setting: Mary is seated, counting her money. Dad enters.)

DAD—What are you doing, Mary?

MARY—I'm counting my money. I have been saving to buy Christmas presents.

DAD—Well, that is great! How much do you have?

MARY—I've got six dollars. Two dollars to spend on you, Mom, and Bill.

DAD—And nothing for yourself?

MARY—No. I want this to be the best Christmas I've ever had. I want to buy the best presents ever!

DAD—Do you want me to take you downtown?

MARY—I am going on the bus. I want the presents to be a real surprise.

Scene II

(Setting: Ragged boy stands on street as though looking through a window. Mary comes in skipping along, humming to herself. Stops and looks at the boy. Begins to go on past and then stops.)

MARY—Say, aren't you Tim Smith who used to live down the street from us?

TIM—Yeah. That's me.

MARY—What are you doing?

TIM—Just looking at the pretty things in the windows. I sure wish I had some money.

MARY—Why didn't you work and earn some? I ran errands and got my money to buy Christmas presents.

TIM—Oh, I've been sick for a long time. I just got to go out the past two weeks.

MARY—Ask your dad for money. He'll give you some.

TIM—I don't have a dad.

MARY—Well, ask your mother.

TIM—Mom's working hard to just get food for me and the other kids. She doesn't have any extra money for stuff like this.

MARY—There should be some way. Well, I've got to do my shopping. Bye, now.

Scene III

(Setting: Mary standing on the street talking to herself.)

MARY—I've looked and looked and I can't make up my mind what to get for my family. I thought that knife might be nice for Bill. Why can't I make up my mind? Oh, dear, here comes Tim again.

TIM—Did you get your presents bought, Mary?

MARY—No, not yet. I can't make up my mind. How many brothers and sisters do you have, Tim?

TIM—I've got twin sisters, who are five, a little brother two and a baby sister one year old. There are five of us. It takes so much money that we probably won't get any Christmas this year at all.

MARY—Say, Tim, I've got an idea. We've got a lot of wood at home that needs to be stacked by the back door for our fireplace. If you would do that you could probably make about six dollars and then you could buy Christmas presents.

Scene IV

(Setting: Tim and Mary meet on the street.)

TIM—Hey, Mary, where are you going?

MARY—I've got to go to the store for Mother. Did you get your shopping done for Christmas?

TIM—I sure did. You can buy a lot with six dollars. I got little doll babies for my twin sisters. I got a truck for my little brother and some pretty blocks for my baby sister.

MARY—Oh, they will love them.

TIM—And guess what else. I had enough to get my mom some perfume. It sure was nice of you to let me stack that wood. I hope your folks didn't mind paying out that six dollars.

MARY—Oh, I'm sure they were glad to get it stacked.

Scene V

(Setting: Mary seated at home.)

DAD—You got your shopping done, did you?

MARY—No, I didn't.

DAD—What is the matter? You sound so gloomy. And do I see a tear?

MARY—Oh, Daddy, I gave my money away to Tim who didn't have any to buy presents with. He stacked the wood and I gave him my six dollars. Now, I don't have any presents for you. *(Begins to cry.)*

DAD—Now, now, Mary. I think you gave us the best present ever, a loving heart. Isn't that what Jesus came into the world for, to bring love and to show us how to love one another?

MARY—You mean you don't care, Daddy?

DAD—You have shown the true spirit of Christmas of loving others. *(Knock at the door. Dad goes to the door.)* Why hello, there, son, come in. *(Tim comes in.)*

TIM—Are you Mary's dad? I'm Tim, and I was the one that stacked the wood for you.

DAD—You did a great job, too.

MARY—Hi, Tim.

TIM—Say, I brought you folks something. Look out there.

DAD—Why Tim, a wagon load of apples. They are beautiful. But didn't they cost a lot of money?

TIM—No, sir. They grow on a tree in our backyard and we save them for winter. This is my Christmas present to Mary and her family.

MARY—Oh, Tim. We love apples. Thank you so much.

TIM—Good-bye now, and Merry Christmas.

DAD and MARY—Good-bye and Merry Christmas to you, too, Tim.

Easter

LEADER—Hello, Johnny, we haven't seen you for a while. Where have you been?

JOHNNY—Just hanging around.

LEADER—Hanging around where?

JOHNNY—In the closet where you left me.

LEADER—Johnny, did you have to tell that? I thought you liked the closet.

JOHNNY—Oh, it's okay. I had time to think up lots of riddles.

LEADER—Well, let's have just one.

JOHNNY—How did Jonah feel when the whale swallowed him?

LEADER—I don't know.

JOHNNY—Down in the mouth. Hey, why do some men wear watches?

LEADER—Why?

JOHNNY—To have a big time. Ha! Ha!

LEADER—Do you know what Sunday this is?

JOHNNY—Sure, it's Easter, but I didn't get a new suit.

LEADER—You don't need a new suit. I don't have one either.

JOHNNY—I thought everyone was supposed to have new clothes for Easter.

LEADER—No; because it is spring, people do get new clothes, but Easter means much more than new clothes.

JOHNNY—I know. It means Jesus' resurrection.

LEADER—That's right. It means Jesus lived and died because He loved us.

JOHNNY—Is Jesus in heaven now?

LEADER—Yes, He is in heaven watching over us all the time.

JOHNNY—You mean He sees all that I do?

LEADER—Of course, and He hears what you say, and even knows what you are thinking. He is God.

JOHNNY—Oh, oh, I had better watch my step. Can He even see inside our house?

LEADER—Yes. But most of all Jesus loves us and wants us to live like true Christians.

JOHNNY—I try to be a good Christian.

LEADER—I know you do and so should we all. I want to please Jesus, too.

JOHNNY—I've got to go now. Remember, boys and girls, live for Jesus every day. Good-bye now.

LEADER—Good-bye, Johnny.

What Easter Meant to Bob

(Play for two boy puppets, one girl)

(Setting: Joe and Mom on way to church.)

JOE—It sure is a nice Easter morning, isn't it, Mom?

SUSIE—Sure is, Joe. It helps me realize more the true meaning of Easter when I see the beautiful flowers.

JOE—Is Jesus really in heaven now?

SUSIE—Of course, Joe. You know that. Jesus rose from the dead many years ago and that is why we have Easter.

JOE—Yeh, I know, but some of the kids make fun and say there isn't any God.

SUSIE—Kids will always do that, Joe, but you have to have faith and believe what the Bible says is true.

JOE—Look, Mom, at that kid over there. Looks like something is wrong.

SUSIE *(goes over to boy)*—What's the matter?

BOB—None of your business.

SUSIE—Has someone hurt you or bothered you in some way?

BOB—Go away. Nobody cares about me. I don't want anyone bothering me, either.

JOE—Hey, kid, I'm Joe, and me and Mom are going to church. Why don't you come along?

BOB—To church! In these old rags? They wouldn't let me near the door.

JOE—Sure they would. None of the guys care about clothes anyway.

SUSIE—We would like for you to go with us. What's your name?

BOB—Bob.

SUSIE—Do you live around here?

BOB—Oh, I hang around where I want to. My mom isn't home much and she doesn't care where I go.

SUSIE—Bob, why don't you come to church and then come home to dinner with us. It's the special Easter service.

BOB—Easter service? What's that?

JOE—You've never heard of Easter? Come on and you'll find out.

BOB—Okay. I guess it's better than hanging around here with nothing to do *(all three leave the stage).*

NARRATOR—And so Joe, his mom, and Bob went to the Easter service. Now the service is over and they are on their way home.

JOE—Hurry up, Bob, let's get going. I can't wait to have some of that big juicy ham for dinner.

BOB—All that stuff the preacher said, is it true?

JOE—Sure, isn't it, Mom?

SUSIE—Sure is. Jesus died on the Cross for our sins and then He arose from the dead and is in heaven right now.

BOB—How do you know that is so, anyway?

SUSIE—Because we believe in the Bible and in Jesus. We've been saved from our sins and our heart tells us it's true.

BOB—My heart doesn't tell me it's true.

JOE—That's because you aren't saved, Bob.

SUSIE—Jesus really does care about you, Bob, and loves you. That's what Easter is all about.

BOB—You mean He knows who I am? No one else does.

SUSIE—He knows you, Bob, and if you would like to give your heart to Jesus, He would save you from your sins and you would be His child.

BOB—Sure would be nice. I don't have a dad and my mom doesn't care much about me.

JOE—It's good to be a Christian. I was saved last year myself.

BOB—What would I tell my mom? She wouldn't like all that foolishness.

SUSIE—Jesus would help you tell her what happened.

JOE—And who knows, maybe she would start loving Jesus, too.

BOB—And maybe she would quit her drinking and running around. Do you suppose?

SUSIE—We would pray about it. We are almost home. Let's go in and have a special prayer. I know that Jesus wants to help you, Bob.

NARRATOR—And so Bob gave his heart to Jesus and became a Christian. Later he told his mother. She began to go to church with him and their home became a happier place. Let's hear Bob's testimony. *(Bob comes back up.)*

BOB—I'm sure glad I became a Christian. It's easy, kids. You ought to let Jesus come into your hearts, too.

Thanksgiving

LEADER—Hello, Johnny.

JOHNNY—Hi! Hi, kids.

LEADER—What have you been doing, Johnny?

JOHNNY—Not much. Hey, do you know why the farmer made the cows sleep on their backs?

LEADER—Why?

JOHNNY—So the cream would be on the top in the morning.

LEADER—Oh, Johnny! Say, how come I saw you up in a tree the other day?

JOHNNY—Well, the sign said, "Keep off the grass."

LEADER—Johnny, you have a lot to learn.

JOHNNY—Say, what is all this about giving thanks? Everywhere today, people are talking about giving thanks. What's the big deal?

LEADER—We are celebrating Thanksgiving this week.

JOHNNY—What does that mean?

LEADER—It means that we should stop and thank God for all the good things He has given us.

JOHNNY—But shouldn't we thank God all of the time?

LEADER—You are so right. God is so good to us that we should never forget to thank Him.

JOHNNY—I have lots of things to be thankful for.

LEADER—What are some of them?

JOHNNY—I am thankful for food, and my clothes and our church and my friends.

LEADER—What about school?

JOHNNY—I don't know if I am thankful for that or not.

LEADER—What about Jesus our Savior?

JOHNNY—Oh, yes, I am glad Jesus came into the world to save us. I am glad all boys and girls can be saved from their sins.

LEADER—And I am thankful, too, that when we die we can go to heaven to be with Jesus.

JOHNNY—Me, too. Boy, I sure have a lot to be thankful for this Thanksgiving. How about you kids?

LEADER—We have to go now, Johnny. Good-bye.

JOHNNY—Good-bye! Good-bye!

On Mother's Day

LEADER—Hi, Johnny. How are you today?

JOHNNY—I'm fine. How are you?

LEADER—Oh, I'm fine. What have you been doing lately?

JOHNNY—I've been learning some elephant jokes. Want to hear one?

LEADER—I guess we can have just one joke.

JOHNNY—Why did the elephant paint his toes red?

LEADER—I don't know. So he could be pretty?

JOHNNY—So he could hide in the strawberry patch. Ha! Ha!

LEADER—That's so silly! What did you get your mother for Mother's Day?

JOHNNY—Well, I saved and saved my money and went to the store to get a present for her.

LEADER—Tell me what you bought.

JOHNNY—A bow and arrow.

LEADER—A bow and arrow for your mother?

JOHNNY—No, for me.

LEADER—What did you buy your mother?

JOHNNY—Nothing. I spent all my money on the bow and arrow. I'm going to let her shoot it, though.

LEADER—Do you think she would like that?

JOHNNY—I think she will. But I'm going to help her with her work this week as a Mother's Day present.

LEADER—Since you spent your money I guess that is the next best thing to do. Just what are you going to do for her?

JOHNNY—First of all I am going to wash the dishes every meal for a whole week.

LEADER—She will love that.

JOHNNY—And then I am going to do everything she tells me the first time she asks.

LEADER—Great, Johnny. I know another present your mother would like, too.

JOHNNY—What's that?

LEADER—Mothers like to hear their little boys and girls say, "I love you," more than anything. And they like lots of kisses and hugs, too.

JOHNNY—Do mothers really like all that mushy stuff? I don't know.

LEADER—They sure do.

JOHNNY—In that case I am going to tell Mother I love her and give her lots of kisses and hugs for Mother's Day.

LEADER—You know mothers do so much for us that we should always remember to show our love to them.

JOHNNY—That's right. I sure couldn't do without my mom.

LEADER—Be sure and let us know next week how your mother liked the bow and arrow.

JOHNNY—I will. Good-bye everyone.

LEADER—Good-bye, Johnny.

Broken Resolutions

(A play for hand puppets or marionettes)

Scene I

(Setting: Betty is seated in the living room.)

BETTY—Now let's see. Here are my New Year's resolutions. First, I'm never going to call my brother bad names when he teases me. Second, I'm going to help with the dishes without Mother asking me several times. Third, I'm going to give an offering every Sunday in Sunday school. This year I'm really going to keep my resolutions.

Scene II

(Setting: Betty seated in living room. Brother Tom comes in.)

TOM—Hi, there, Kid. Where did you get that ugly face?

Silence

47

Tom—Didn't you hear me, ugly face? Boy, if your face would freeze like that you would scare even the witches. Ha! Ha!

Silence

Tom—What's the matter? Cat got your tongue? Cat got your tongue?

Betty—Oh, Tom, I hate you. You are so mean, mean, mean, mean!

Tom—Ugly face, ugly face.

Betty—I hate you. You are a no-good, mean brother. That's what you are.

Scene III

(Setting: Betty is reading a book.)

Voice from Offstage—Betty, it's the middle of the afternoon. Aren't you going to do the dishes?

Betty—In a little while, Mother.

Voice—Betty, you said that a long time ago. You had better do the dishes now.

Betty—Oh, all right *(stomps off)*.

Scene IV

(Setting: Pastor is seated in his study. A knock is heard.)

Pastor *(goes to door)*—Why, hello, Betty. Come in.

Betty—Hello, Pastor Jones.

Pastor—What can I do for you today, Betty?

Betty—I sure have got a problem.

Pastor—Just after Christmas and you have a problem.

Betty—You see, I made these New Year's resolutions and said I was going to be good all year long and here the year is just getting started and I've already broken some of my resolutions.

Pastor—Tell me about it.

Betty—Well, I said I wouldn't call my brother names and he teased me. I got mad and told him I hated him.

Pastor—I see. What else happened?

Betty—And then I said I would do the dishes without Mother asking me to so much, and then just the other day, I read my book and didn't get the dishes done till the middle of the afternoon after Mother had asked me several times.

Pastor—Anything else?

BETTY—Yes. I said I wasn't going to use my Sunday school money for anything but Sunday school. But the other day when I was with my friends, they all bought sodas. And the only money I had left was for Sunday school. So I used it to buy a soda, too.

PASTOR—Betty, you are trying to do all of those things by yourself. You need to let Jesus come into your heart. Let Him become your Savior and Helper. Then He will help you do right.

BETTY—But I do go to church, Pastor Jones.

PASTOR—It is more than going to church. It is letting Jesus become a part of our lives. It is letting Him control our lives and Him helping us not to sin and to live a good life.

BETTY—Oh, I want Jesus to come into my life.

PASTOR—Let's kneel down and pray. You ask Him to forgive you of your sins and come into your life. And He will.

BETTY—Dear Jesus, please forgive me of the bad things I have done. I am sorry that I have sinned. Please come into my life and help me to be good and to live for You. Amen.

PASTOR—Dear Lord, we thank you for listening to our prayer today. Help Betty to live for you every day as a Christian should. Amen.

BETTY—I feel so much better. I did let Jesus come in and I know He is going to help me live a good life.

PASTOR—Now, Betty, remember to pray every day and to trust Jesus to help you. Read your Bible every day, too.

BETTY—I will, Pastor. And thank you for helping me. Good-bye.

PASTOR—Good-bye, Betty.

Vacation Time

(For boy and girl sack puppets)

SAM—Hi, Sue.

SUE—Hi, Sam.

SAM—Say, Sue, I sure want to get my name changed.

SUE—How come?

SAM—Because my dad says he is going to spank me as sure as my name is Sam.

SUE—I know a better one than that. My dad can't decide whether to get a tractor or a cow.

SAM—He had better get a tractor. He sure would look silly riding around on a cow.

SUE—But he would look sillier milking a tractor.

SAM—What do you want to do this summer? School is almost out, you know.

SUE—We are going to take a trip and we are going to visit a different church every Sunday.

SAM—Aw, what do you want to go to church for on vacation?

SUE—You know we are supposed to be in church every Sunday, even in the summer.

SAM—But if you were away no one would know if you were in church or not.

SUE—God would know. We go to church, anyway, to worship God, not to please people.

SAM—Yeh, but look at the time you'll waste when you could be having fun.

SUE—My mother says that time spent in church is good for us. It helps us to relax and think of God and all the good things He does for us.

SAM—Maybe she's right. I guess you think I should go to church every Sunday even if I'm home.

SUE—Yes, I do. God doesn't take a vacation from helping us, does He?

SAM—No, He doesn't. I guess I should keep prayed up in case I need God to help us during our vacation.

SUE—God says to call on Him when we are in trouble, even on vacation.

SAM—I am going to church every Sunday this summer. And something else. I'm going to keep up on my prayers. I don't want to be caught not on speaking terms with God.

SUE—Me, too. We'll see you around, Sam.

SAM—See you, too. Good-bye.

Fourth of July

JOHNNY—Bang! Bang! Bang!

LEADER—Johnny, what are you doing?

JOHNNY—I'm getting ready for the Fourth of July. I'm gonna shoot off guns and firecrackers.

LEADER—Don't you know that could be dangerous?

JOHNNY—But isn't that what we are supposed to do?

LEADER—We are celebrating our country's independence but we don't shoot guns anymore, or firecrackers. They are dangerous.

JOHNNY—You mean I might get shot or hurt?

LEADER—Lots of boys get shot playing with guns.

JOHNNY—Firecrackers can't hurt, can they?

LEADER—Some have gotten their hands blown off and their eyes put out.

JOHNNY—Really! Maybe you're right. But I sure want to celebrate the Fourth of July.

LEADER—You can. We can go over to the park after it gets dark. They are going to have big, big, big fireworks. Colored lights and rockets and everything.

JOHNNY—Oh, boy, that will be fun. What else?

LEADER—I tell you what. I will make a big Fourth of July cake and we can put lights on it and celebrate the birthday of our country.

JOHNNY—Can I invite some friends, too?

LEADER—Of course. We'll have hot dogs and cake for supper and then in the evening we can go to the park.

JOHNNY—That will be great!

LEADER—You know, we don't want to take a chance on firecrackers or guns because someone might get hurt and that wouldn't be pleasing to God.

JOHNNY—No, I sure wouldn't want to hurt anyone. I'll see you around, kids!

LEADER—We'll see you, Johnny. Good-bye.